Developing Interpersonal Skills

90 Minute Guides

Michelle N. Halsey

Silver City Publications & Training, L.L.C.
P.O. Box 1914
Nampa, ID 83653
https://www.silvercitypublications.com/shop/

ISBN-10: 1-64004-018-8
ISBN-13: 978-1-64004-018-2

Contents

Chapter 1 – Verbal Communication Skills

We've all met that dynamic, charismatic person that just has a way with others, and has a way of being remembered. This workshop will help participants work towards being that unforgettable person by providing communication skills, negotiation techniques, tips on making an impact, and advice on networking and starting conversations.

By the end of this tutorial, participants will be able to:

- Understand the difference between hearing and listening

- Know some ways to improve the verbal skills of asking questions and communicating with power.

- Understand what non-verbal communication is and how it can enhance interpersonal relationships.

- Identify the skills needed in starting a conversation, moving a conversation along, and progressing to higher levels of conversation.

- Identify ways of creating a powerful introduction, remembering names, and managing situations when you've forgotten someone's name.

- Understand how seeing the other side, building bridges and giving in without giving up can improve skills in influencing other people.

- Understand how the use of facts and emotions can help bring people to your side.

- Identify ways of sharing one's opinions constructively.

- Learn tips in preparing for a negotiation, opening a negotiation, bargaining, and closing a negotiation.

- Learn tips in making an impact through powerful first impressions, situation assessment, and being zealous without being offensive.

As a pre-assignment, think of a social situation that you consider most stressful. This situation can be within an employment, community, family, or recreational setting. Example: introducing one's self to strangers.

After coming up with the social situation you find most stressful, answer the following questions:

- What aspect of this situation do you find most stressful? Why?

- What do you think are the interpersonal skills needed in order to successfully navigate this situation? List down at least three.

- On a scale of 1 to 5, with 1 being the least effective and 5 being the most, rate your effectiveness in practicing the skills you listed.

- Looking at your responses, which skills do you practice most effectively? What helps you in practicing these skills well?

- Which skills do you practice least effectively? What keeps you from practicing these skills well?

Words are powerful tools of communication. Indeed, word choice can easily influence the thoughts, attitudes, and behavior of the people listening to us. Similarly, proper attention to the language of others can give us insight to what it is that they are *really* saying, helping us to respond appropriately and effectively.

In this module, we will discuss important verbal communication skills like the art of listening, asking questions, and communicating with power.

Listening and Hearing: They Aren't the Same Thing

Most people can hear, but few can really listen.

Hearing is simply the process of perceiving sounds within our environment. The best way to illustrate hearing is through the biological processes involved in sensory perception. Specifically: our ears pick up sound waves around us, sends signals to our brain, and our brain in turn tells us what the sound is and where it is coming from.

Listening, on the other hand, goes beyond simply picking up stimuli around us, and identifying what these stimuli are. Listening involves the extra steps of really understanding what we heard, and giving it deliberate attention and thoughtful consideration. It may be said that listening involves a more active participation from a person than simply hearing.

Here is an example to illustrate the difference between hearing and listening:

A secretary entered her boss' office and presented her boss with a copy of the schedule for the next day. The secretary told the boss that she has a packed day for tomorrow, and that she only has an hour of break time for the whole afternoon.

The boss, busy studying a report, merely nodded to the secretary, and motioned for her to place the schedule on her desk. The boss continued to study the report as if there were no interruption. In this case, the boss simply heard what the secretary said; the boss paid just enough attention to make an appropriate but non-committal reaction.

Had the boss been listening, her reaction would have been different.

She would have set aside the report she was reading and paid 100% attention to what the secretary was saying. She could also have processed the implication of the message. For instance, upon learning that she has a packed day ahead, she could have arranged for her lunch to be delivered, or noted to herself that she needs to get a good night's sleep.

Taking the extra step to move from hearing to listening can enhance a person's interpersonal relationships in many ways. Listening promotes a more accurate and deeper understanding of a person's communication, helping a responder to provide the most appropriate response. But more so, when you're listening to a person, you communicate to them that you value not just what they are saying, but their presence as well.

Asking Questions

If communication is the exchange of information between two or more people, then questions are a way to elicit the specific information that you are looking for. But more so, well-crafted questions make for an engaging conversation. It can establish rapport, spark interest, and curiosity in others, break new grounds, and communicate your own sincerity in learning what people around you have to say.

Here are some tips in asking questions effectively:

Ask! First of all, don't be afraid to ask questions! Sometimes shyness, concern over making a faux pas, or fear of being perceived as a busybody, can keep us from asking questions. While some subject matters are not appropriate conversation pieces in the early stages of a conversation (we will discuss this later, in the section on Levels of Conversation), there's nothing wrong in asking questions per se. Start with your inherent curiosity about people, if you're genuinely interested in a person, you won't run out of things to ask.

Ask open questions. There are two kinds of questions based on the scope of the answers they elicit: closed and open questions.

- Closed questions are questions answerable by yes or no. Example: "Are you happy with today's presentation?"

- Open questions, on the other hand, are questions that require a qualified response. Open questions are usually preceded by who, when, where, what, how, and why. Example: "What is it about today's presentation that you find most engaging?"

- Open questions are more effective than closed questions because they evoke thoughtful consideration of the subject and creative thinking.

Ask purposeful questions. There are different reasons why we ask questions, and it is important that we take note of our purpose in asking a question. Doing so can help us frame our questions better, and keep the questions relevant.

For example, we can ask questions with the goal of making the other person feel at ease. Questions like these should be phrased in a pleasant, non-threatening manner, and involves subjects that the other person is likely to be interested in. Example: *"That's a lovely blouse! Where did you get it?"*

Some questions are designed to challenge the other person's thinking, and encourage a lively debate or deliberation. Questions like these should be phrased in a way that is focused and process-oriented. It can also challenge existing assumptions about the subject matter. Example: *"How do you think a leader can better motivate his team?"*

In other times, questions are meant to encourage a person to join an existing discussion. The goal of these questions is to invite participation, as much as gain information. Example: *"I find Matthew's approach very refreshing. What do you think, Frank?"*

For better effectiveness, think of what you and the person you're talking to needs in your stage of relationship, and ask him or her questions that can address that need.

Communicating with Power

Power in communication refers to the ability to influence, persuade, or make an impact. A powerful communication is associated with self-confidence, credibility, and effectiveness.

The following are some ways you can communicate with power verbally:

Stick to the point. Powerful communication is not about saying as many things as you can in a given period of time. Rather, it is about sticking to what is relevant to the discussion, and getting your message across in the shortest --- but most impact-laden --- way possible. Get rid of fillers like *"uhm…"*, *"you know"*, or *"actually"* in your delivery, and avoid off-topic statements. Just provide the bare bones --- the ideas your audience would be most interested in knowing, or the ones that promote your intentions best.

Don't be too casual. Note that phrasing appropriate when talking with friends is not necessarily appropriate for business-related meets. The use of slang, street talk, and poor grammar can detract from your credibility, especially if you're mingling with potential clients, employers, and business partners. Events that require you to come across as impressive may require the use of industry-specific jargon and a formal tone --- so adjust accordingly.

Emphasize key ideas. Stress the highlights of your communication. For example, people who are delivering a sales pitch should emphasize the main features of their product or service. Those who are presenting their opinion on an issue should explain the crux of their arguments, and build from there. Even if you're merely expressing interest or congratulations, make sure the person you're talking to would remember what you have to say. Emphasis in verbal communication comes in many ways, including repetition of key points, giving specific examples, accenting particular adjectives or nouns, or even directly saying that "this is really a point I want to emphasize."

Tailor-fit your communication to your audience. A powerful communication is one that connects with one's audience. In this case, minding the readiness, attention, age, and educational level of your audience is very important, so that you don't overwhelm or underwhelm them. Social skills are primarily about flexibility; the better you can adjust to changes in your audience profile, the better off you'll be.

Connect. Power in communication is sometimes determined by the quality of your rapport with others. You may need to "warm up" your audience, make them comfortable, and show them that you sincerely want to talk with them. The more others see you as "one of them", the better their reception of anything that you have to say will be.

Your non-verbal communication can be a big help in connecting with others.

Chapter 2 – Non-Verbal Communication Skills

Communication is not just about what comes out of our mouths. In fact, what we don't say --- our body language, voice intonation and use of silence ---- often sends a louder message to other people than the words we say. Unless we actively practice non-verbal communication skills, we can't really be sure if we're actually sending the message that we want to send.

Body Language

Body language refers to the messages we send to other people through our posture, facial expression, gestures, and bodily movements.

It is believed that a listener pays more attention to body language than verbal messages. This implies that if one's body language is inconsistent with the verbal message being sent (e.g. frowning while saying you're happy), the verbal message becomes less credible. In fact, such inconsistency can even nullify the verbal message, and result to the verbal message being perceived as a lie. At the very least, inconsistencies between verbal and non-verbal communication can result in confusion.

The following are some of the components of body language:

Eye Contact: Eye contact is considered one of the most important aspects of non-verbal communication. Steady eye contact often indicates attention to the person one is in conversation with, as well as a willingness and sincerity to connect. The lack of eye connect can be viewed as defensiveness, nervousness and or social withdrawal. Many say that our eyes are the "windows to our soul", and that one can tell if an individual is happy, sad, or angry simply by looking at their eyes.

Facial Expression: It is believed that there are universal facial expressions for different emotions, most of which have an evolutionary basis. For example, anger is often indicated by sharp stares, crunched eyebrows and the baring of teeth. Sadness, on the other hand, can be denoted by teary eyes and drooping lips. Note though that the expression and perception of emotions tend to vary from culture to culture.

Posture: The way we sit down, stand up or even walk can also communicate. For example, slumping in a chair is often considered as a sign of inattention and or disrespect. Walking with one's head and shoulders down can be interpreted as a sign of nervousness or low self-esteem. Withdrawing to a fetal position can also be indicative of fear and or depression. The puffing of one's chest has been traditionally interpreted as pride.

Specific Movements: There are specific movements that have traditionally been associated with certain messages. For example, nodding is generally a sign of assent or agreement. Raising clenched hands are interpreted as a sign of angry challenge. Stomping our feet can be an indication of frustration.

Physical Contact: The way we physically interact with other people is also a part of body language. Shaking of hands, hugging, slapping, punching are forms of communication. The same can be said about our physical closeness and distance with another person. Standing too close to a person can be considered as an invasion of boundaries, while standing too far from a person can be construed as avoidance.

The Signals You Send to Others

Generally, our non-verbal communication is something that we do unconsciously. It can be influenced by many things, including past habits, life experiences, personal models, culture and hidden thoughts and feelings. Because body language is often outside of awareness, most have no idea what it is exactly that they are communicating to other people.

To take control of the signals that we send to others, it's important that we become much more deliberate and purposive in communicating non-verbally.

The following are some tips and techniques you can follow to be able to use body language effectively.

Increase your awareness of your body language. Try to get more information about what you communicate non-verbally, so that you will know what to change and what to retain. Ways you can do this include: watching a videotape of yourself, studying yourself in front of a mirror, and getting feedback from peers and friends.

Know how certain behaviors are typically interpreted. Interpreting body language can be very subjective. There are, however, typical interpretations to specific body language. Increasing awareness of what body language is often associated with what interpretation, can help a person avoid body language incongruent with the message they want to send; as well as deliberately practice the body language congruent with their message.

Practice! Practice! Practice! Body language is a skill. Initially, using body language that is congruent with the message that we want to communicate will feel unnatural. But just keep on working on it. Soon, it'll be second nature to you!

It's Not What You Say, It's How You Say It

Non-verbal communication also includes the way we deliver information. A simple change in tone and inflection can change the meaning of statements. It is important then, to be aware of the way we speak, so that we can communicate more effectively.

The following are aspects of "how we say things" that we should take note of:

Tone of Voice: Voice intonation refers to the use of changing pitch in order to convey a message. The same message, for example, can be delivered using a rising intonation, a dipping intonation, or a falling intonation. Changes in tone can help inject emotions into messages; messages can be upbeat or depressing depending on the speaker's tone. Changes in tone can also help identify what is the purpose of a sentence. There are intonations that better fit a question, and intonations that better fit a declarative sentence.

Stress and Emphasis: Changing which words or syllables you put emphasis on can change its meaning. For example, consider the differences among these three statements below. The italicized word represents where the emphasis is.

- You mean *he* disobeyed his mother?

- You mean he *disobeyed* his mother?

- You mean he disobeyed *his mother*?

Pace and Rhythm: The speed of speech, as well as the appropriate use of pauses can change the meaning of words spoken, and affect the clarity and effectiveness of a communication. For instance, people who speak too fast can be difficult to talk to --- a listener might feel too pressured to catch everything that they have to say! On the other hand, a person who speaks too slowly can bore their listener.

Volume: How softly and how loudly you speak also matters in communication. Ideally, one should generally speak in a moderate volume while in the company of others; a too soft voice can communicate nervousness or lack of assertiveness, while a loud voice can communication anger and aggression. A person should also be flexible, able to whisper or shout when it's appropriate to do so.

Pronunciation and Enunciation. How well a message comes across is influenced by pronunciation and enunciation. Pronunciation refers to speaking a word in a way that's generally accepted or understood, while enunciation is the act of speaking clearly and concisely. Developing one's skills in pronunciation and enunciation ensures that one is accurately understood. Note that accents can cause varieties in what is considered as acceptable pronunciation.

Chapter 3 – Making Small Talk and Moving Beyond

Small talk is the "ice-breaking" part of a conversation; it is the way strangers can ease into comfortable rapport with one another. Mastering the art of small talk ---- and how to build from this stage--- can open many personal and professional doors. In this module, we will discuss how to start a conversation, as well as how to skillfully ease our conversation starters into deeper levels of talk.

Starting a Conversation

Many people are interested in initiating friendships and productive business networks, but they don't know how to start. Indeed, going up to a stranger and making an introduction can be incredibly anxiety-provoking for some people. The same goes with finding something to talk about with someone you already know, but are not familiar with.

The following are some tips in starting a conversation:

Understand what holds you back. The first step in developing conversation skills is to understand what factors --- attitudes, feelings, and assumptions --- interfere in your ability to skillfully handle a conversation. Is it shyness? Fear of rejection? Difficulty in dealing with people in authority? Awareness of what holds you back can help you manage your anxieties better, and give you more control over how you handle yourself during social situations.

Know what you have to offer. In the same way that you have to make an inventory of your weaknesses during social situations, you also have to take stock of your strengths. Confidence in initiating conversations does not begin with knowing what tried-and-tested lines are out there. It starts with a sincere belief that you have something to contribute to a discussion, and that people would find it a pleasant experience to get to know you. If you have this self-assurance, you can be more at ease and more natural around other people.

Be interested about people. Genuine curiosity and openness makes starting a conversation less threatening; it grants incentive to approach people.

Cultivate the attitude that meeting people is an enriching experience. It shouldn't be that hard; this mantra goes beyond self-talk. Many find that you can actually learn a lot about yourself, about life and about various subject matters, just by simply engaging in constant conversation. And remember: being interested in people doesn't end after you've spent time with them. Even those you've spent years with can still tell you something you don't know!

Create an arsenal of conversation starters. For people not used to skillfully handling conversations, the first few tries can feel awkward. While you're still finding your footing, you can rely on some recommended conversation starters. Among them are:

- Introduce yourself. The most straightforward way to start a conversation is to offer your name and your hand. By making the first move in breaking silence, you're sending the other person an invitation into conversation. If you can make the introduction with a smile, better.

- Comment on something in your immediate surroundings, maybe the location, or the event you both are attending. Things that you both can relate with are good conversation starters, as it does not alienate anyone. Example: "It's really crowded tonight, isn't it?"

- Comment on something the other person or people would find interesting. For example, if you're talking with someone known for his or her art collection, you may call attention to an art piece within your vicinity, or inform him about an exhibit you heard about. Example: "Hey Bob, I just heard that the National Museum is hosting a Renaissance week." And if you have no prior knowledge about the person you want to strike a conversation with, you can take a guess at their interests by subtly checking what they are looking at, or studying their appearance. Example: *"That's a lovely brooch. It looks like an antique."*

- **Relax.** *"Be yourself"* is generally good advice for handling social situations. Conversations are more comfortable and engaging if participants simply relax, and let their personalities do the talking. Don't pressure yourself coming up with something funny, clever, or new. Scripts are okay while you're still developing your social skills, but make sure you also give conversations your personal touch!

The Four Levels of Conversation

The real art of conversation is not only to say the right thing at the right place, but to leave unsaid the wrong thing at tempting moment. It requires sensitivity to the stage of a relationship, the context of the conversation and the comfort level of the person you are talking to.

There are 4 levels of conversation based on the degree and amount of personal disclosure. They are:

Level 1: Small Talk: This is commonly referred to as the 'exchange of pleasantries' stage. In this level, you talk only about generic topics, subjects that almost everyone is comfortable discussing. These subjects include the weather, the location you're both in and current events.

The small talk stage establishes rapport; it makes a person feel at ease with you. It's also a safe and neutral avenue for people to subtly 'size up' one another, and explore if it's a conversation or relationship that they'd want to invest in.

If the small talk goes well, you can proceed into the next level: fact disclosure.

Level 2: Fact Disclosure: In this stage, you tell the other person some facts about you such as your job, your area of residence, and your interests.

This is a 'getting-to-know' stage, and it aims to see if you have something in common with the other person. It's also a signal that you are opening up a little bit to the other person while still staying on neutral topics.

If the fact disclosure stage goes well, you can proceed to sharing viewpoints and opinions.

Level 3: Viewpoints and Opinions: In this stage of the conversation, you can offer what you think about various topics like politics, the new business model ---or even the latest blockbuster. It helps then to read and be curious about many things, from politics to entertainment to current events.

Sharing viewpoints and opinions require the 'buffering effect' of the first two stages for two reasons:

- First, a person needs rapport with another before they can discuss potentially contentious statements, even if they're having a healthy debate.

- Second, sharing viewpoints and opinions opens a person to the scrutiny of another, and this requires that there is some level of safety and trust in a relationship.

The controversial, and therefore potentially offensive, nature of an opinion exists in a range; make sure that you remain within the 'safe' zone in the early stages of your relationship.

Level 4: Personal Feelings: The fourth stage is disclosure and acknowledgment of personal feelings. For instance you can share about your excitement for the new project, or your worry about your son's upcoming piano recital. Depending on the context and the level of the friendship, you can disclose more personal subjects. This stage requires trust, rapport, and even a genuine friendship, because of the intimate nature of the subject.

Different people have different comfort levels when it comes to disclosing feelings, and there are cases when you'd need several conversations before they would trust enough to open themselves. In some cases, you never get to this stage. Just make sure to be sensitive and test the other person's readiness before opening an intimate topic.

Listening is vital in all stages of the conversation but especially so in this fourth stage. Listen with empathy and understanding to acknowledge that you heard the feeling that they have shared.

Moving the Conversation Along

Initiating a conversation is one interpersonal skill, maintaining it is another. An engaging and effective conversation is one that "flows" and "goes forward." To be able to keep a conversation from being stuck, it's best to know techniques in moving a conversation along. In this module we will discuss techniques like asking for examples, using repetition, using summary questions, and asking for clarity and completeness.

Asking for Examples

One way to get a conversation partner to elaborate on what they are sharing with you is to ask for examples. Examples make a specific general statement, and give an insight on the particulars of a disclosure. It can also serve to illustrate principles shared, or personalize an experience.

The following conversation excerpts illustrate how asking for examples can move a conversation along:

Excerpt 1

Person A: C.S. Lewis is one of my all-time favorite writers.

Person B: C.S. Lewis? I am not familiar with his work. *Could you give an example of what he has done?*

Person A: Well, he wrote the Chronicles of Narnia. It's a children's series with seven books. I find it very inspiring.

Excerpt 2

Person A: This is a great company to work for. They really care about their employees.

Person B: *In what ways do they care for the staff?*

Person A: Well, their medical aid program is a good example of how they prioritize health and security. All ABC Company employees are registered with a private insurance firm from their first day of work.

Person B: Wow. That's very generous. *In what other ways are they employee-oriented?*

Person A: The staff members are also scheduled for an annual week-long retreat, all expenses paid for by the company.

Using Repetition

Questions are not the only powerful tools that you can use to keep a conversation going. Repeating certain words, phrases, or even statements that a person discloses to you can also maintain the momentum of your talk, or urge it to a new direction.

In what way can repetition keep a conversation going?

Repetition can be a way of saying *"please go on"* or *"tell me more."* It is a technique of acknowledging that you have heard what the other person said, and or something about their disclosure has picked your attention. It is an encouragement for them to elaborate.

Repetition is also a way of focusing a conversation on an interesting aspect. Your choice of what word, phrase, or statement to repeat will signal to the other person what you'd like to hear more about. One way you can use this technique to your advantage is to repeat a word, phrase or statement that you feel has a lot more story to it. You may also zero in on what you think the other person likes to talk about more, or what you yourself find intriguing.

Lastly, repetition can also be a way of communicating your reaction to what the other person said. Varying the intonation and pitch of your voice can inject your repetition with emotions of surprise, shock, excitement, or confusion.

The following conversation excerpts illustrate how repetition can move a conversation along:

Excerpt 1:

Person A: Mark and I have been married for 40 years now. We'll be renewing our vows in April.

Person B: *Forty years.*

Person A: Yes. Amazing, isn't it? It wasn't always easy but we made it through. Very few people who married the same time as us are still together now. I know I am one of the lucky ones.

Excerpt 2:

Person A: I can't believe it! The guys threw me a surprise party.

Person B: *The guys threw you a birthday party.*

Person A: Yes! It really made my day.

Note that in repetition you don't necessarily have to repeat the same exact phase. You can make changes necessary to make the repetition more effective.

Using Summary Questions

Another way to keep a conversation moving is to summarize what has been discussed, or what you heard from the other person, every now and then.

A summary can communicate that you are really listening, and that you have taken stock of everything the other person has said. More so, it gives a sense of movement to the conversation, because summaries say that one part of the conversation is over, and that it's time to move on to another part.

Note that in repetition you don't necessarily have to repeat the same exact phase. You can make changes necessary to make the repetition more effective.

The following conversation excerpts illustrate how summary questions can move a conversation along:

Excerpt 1:

Person A: I'm really geared up for this coming marathon! I changed my diet, hired a trainer, and I've been practicing 3-4 hours a day. I've never felt more in shape; I feel that I have a real shot at winning this!

Person B: *You're really invested in this marathon; you really think you have a chance to win?*

Person A: Yes. Amazing, isn't it!

Excerpt 2:

Person A: I want this project to be the one of the most successful for this trimester. We've had a run of bad luck the past month, and we need a big break to recoup it all. Judging by the projections the accounting department made, I think we're right on track!

Person B: That's great! How can I help?

Person A: We need a design person. You're good at art, right? Can you make us a logo?

Person B: Sure. Just give me the specs you want and I'm on it.

Person A: And a pamphlet as well? One that has all of the company colors in it. Same with the logo!

Person B: No problem. *Let me see if I understood you right. You need a pamphlet and a logo with the company colors in it. Is this correct?*

Person A: That's it. Thanks!

Asking for Clarity and Completeness

Here's another way of moving a conversation along: asking for clarity and completeness.

It is important to verify your understanding of a communication, and see if you have accurate and or complete information. Often, a speaker presumes that he or she is understood, and therefore tends to miss on certain details. They may think that they have the same frame of reference with the other person, and consequently does not need to expand on the meaning of their statements. At times, intense emotions, like excitement can result in lack of clarity and completeness in communication.

Asking for clarity and completeness can give your conversation depth and richness of idea. It can also communicate your sincere desire to understand what the other person is saying.

The following conversation excerpt illustrates how asking for clarity and completeness can move a conversation along:

Excerpt 1:

Person A: My 7-year old daughter wants to become an actress! She's been begging me to enroll her in this intensive acting community workshop, but I'm afraid it will just spoil her.

Person B: *I don't understand. What do you mean by 'it will just spoil her'?*

Person A: You know…I think it will indulge her too much. I want her to grow up disciplined by school and household chores. I don't want her to be like many young stars nowadays, who don't seem to know what's real and what's not.

Person B: *I think I understand what you mean. Are you saying that she'll miss the normal demands of everyday that keeps people grounded?*

Person A: Exactly!

Remembering Names

Writer and lecturer Dale Carnegie once said that *"a person's name to him or her is the sweetest and most important sound in any language."* When we address people by name, we are telling them that we respect them, consider them as important, recognize their individuality, and warmly relate with them. If you want to be able to cultivate many functional friendships and working partnerships, you need the ability of remembering names.

Creating a Powerful Introduction

Three steps to introducing yourself effectively:

Step 1: Project warmth and confidence. Many people size you up even before you say a word, which is why it's important to mind your body language. When you introduce yourself, stand up straight, relax, and establish eye contact.

Step 2: State your first name and your last name. Depending on the situation, you may also state your affiliation and or your position in the company. Example: *"Hello. I'm Jacqueline Smith. I'm the Quality Control Officer."*

Step 3: When the other person has given their name, repeat it in acknowledgment. *"It's nice to meet you, Mr. Andrews."* or *"It's nice to meet you, Joseph."* Repeating their name is an acknowledgment that you heard their introduction.

Using Mnemonics

One technique that has been known to work in helping improve recall is the use of mnemonic devices. Mnemonic devices are ways of conceptualizing ideas that aim to organize arbitrary things into meaningful data. Things that seem random are harder to remember; mnemonic devices help organize ideas in our minds.

Here are examples of mnemonic devices you can use in name recall:

Clustering by Categories: Grouping the items that you need to remember into categories can help you remember them better. For example, to memorize a list of contacts, group them by company or by profession.

Visualizing Interactive Images: Some people memorize better when they create a scene in their heads where all the items that they have to remember are interacting with each other in some active way. For example, if you have to remember to Mark, Joseph and Martha, imagine a Biblical Joseph being served tea by Martha Stewart while he's playing target shooting (the bulls-eye can remind you of the synonym "mark")

Acronyms: This is a method where you devise a word or expression in which each of its letters stand for a name. An example is SALE for Sally, Andrew, Louise and Ester

Acrostics: This mnemonic device follows the same logic as acronyms except that one forms a sentence rather than a single word to help one remember new words. For example one might remember 'all babies cry loudly' for Allan, Betty, Chris and Lisa.

Uh-Oh…I've Forgotten Your Name

Most of us have been there before: a situation when someone says "hi" to us, but we have absolutely no idea who is talking to us. At best we'd just feel awkward and embarrassed; at worse, we might end up offending the other person. To better manage situations like this, it is recommended that you:

- Understand why you forget names. Often, forgetting names is not about memory problems --- it's about attitude problems. Perhaps you don't think remembering names is important. Maybe you don't trust your ability to manage a list of names in your head. Or it's possible that you get easily nervous in social situations, you tend to mentally blank out. Identify what holds you back from remembering people's name. Exert a deliberate effort to improve your rate of name recall. It is only when you have an open attitude that name recall becomes easy.

- Ask a third party. One way you can avoid showing your memory lapse is to seek a third person's help subtly. If you see a face in a crowd that looks familiar, but whose name you can't recall, ask a friend: "Hey, do you know the woman at the back?" A little research prior to walking up to a person can help you prevent a potentially embarrassing situation.

- Ask for a card. Asking for a calling card can be a way to subtly get the other person's name. For example, you can say: *"Hey, I don't think I have your card yet, here's mine."*

- Introduce other people to them. If you have people you know around you, why don't you initiate an introduction? For instance you can say "Hey, have you met my friend Mark? Mark is a PR in this company." Politeness would typically compel the person to introduce himself or herself to Mark, and you can catch their name at that point.

- Be honest. And if you really can't recall who the person is, and the other person appears amiable enough, then perhaps you can come clean. You can say: *"I'm sorry; I know that we've met, but I seem to have forgotten your name."* You may also add some details that you do remember, to ease the effect of your memory loss. *"We met at the company dinner, right, last September? You were with your lovely children."* Hopefully, the other person can empathize with your distress and re-introduce themselves.

Chapter 4 – Influencing Skills

The skill of influencing others is a valuable asset to have; it can help us sell products and ideas, convince people and institutions to assist us, and even get the world to change! After all, while we don't have the power to control other people, we can always do our best to persuade them.

In this module, we will discuss how to improve our influencing skills. Particularly, we will discuss techniques like seeing the other side, building a bridge and giving in without giving up.

Seeing the Other Side

The first step in influencing other people is entering their world. This means setting aside your own point of view, and looking at the situation from another person's perspective. Remember, each person is unique, and consequently sees the world differently. You can't always assume that what's clear to you is clear to the people you are talking to.

In short, you have to be able to answer this question for them: *"what's in it for me?"*

Seeing the other side involves knowing what is important to the other person(s): their values, interests, and preferences. Do they have strong feelings against what you are pitching to them? What would it take to for them to get over their resistance? What are their characteristics, personality traits, social status, or professions that can you use in order to make your point more convincing?

Research, active listening, and keen observation can help you in "seeing the other side."

Consider this example:

How do you convince city-based, working mothers to plant medicinal plants instead of buying factory-made pharmaceuticals?

If you are not practicing the skill of "seeing the other side", you might be tempted to argue that having medicines readily available in the home is more convenient than having to run to the pharmacy every time someone is sick.

But this argument may not be so convincing if you consider the world city-based working mothers live in. As city-dwellers with full time jobs, working mothers would likely find buying from the pharmacy much more convenient than finding space in an urban home for plants. More so, the demand of having to water the plants and expose them to sunlight every day is too much added responsibility.

On the other hand, mothers would always respond to one prime value ---- their child's health and welfare. If you can present a case on how pollution in the city and chemical-based food and drugs lower resistance to diseases among children, and that natural medicines are both a way to improve kids' health and show love, you may be able to build a stronger case for planting medicinal plants at home.

Building a Bridge

A second skill that can help you during situations that need persuasion is bridge building.

Bridge building is the process of increasing rapport and affinity between people. It can involve making the other party feel at ease talking to you, gaining their trust, and identifying common interests.

Bridge building is important in persuasion because people are more likely to agree with someone they like, trust, or see as "one of them." Aside from bridges improving the over-all communication between two parties, bridges can also serve as negotiating grounds. Bridges translate to common interests, which can be the foundation of win-win scenarios.

The following are some of the ways you can build bridges in your interpersonal relationships:

Active Listening. If you want to gain another person's trust, you have to communicate that you value their presence, and that you are exerting the effort to understand what they are saying to you. Listening attentively is a way to do this.

Use Common Language. An indirect way of building bridges is showing by your words, manner of speaking and even by body language, that you are one with the other person. For example, use business language when you're speaking with the company CEO, but use laymen terms when speaking with blue-collared workers. Pay attention to how the other person phrases his statements; if they're formal, be formal, and if they're casual, then follow suit. Similarly, attend to their pace of doing business. Some people like to relax before a deal, others like to go straight to business. Adjust your approach accordingly.

Highlight Similarities. No matter how differently two people appear they will always have at least one thing in common. If you want to persuade a person, find these areas of similarities and emphasize them. An important similarity to emphasize is common interests --- goals that you both share, that the proposal you're pitching can address. The previous skill of "seeing the other side" can assist you in this process.

Sustained Communication. Lastly, consistent and sustained communication about matters of interest can help you in influencing other people. If you feel that there is significant resistance to you or to your proposal, or there are marked differences between you and the other person, just persistently meet with the person and open communication lines. Sometimes, your mere visibility in another person's circle can increase your likeability and credibility.

Giving In Without Giving Up

Issues are rarely black and white. In most cases, there are areas within a contention that you can compromise upon. If you want to improve your chances of influencing other people, be willing to make some concessions ---- even if it's just at the levels of simply agreeing to differ, agreeing that the other person has a right to their opinion, or agreeing that the other person has made a reasonable argument.

The skill of giving in is important because people generally don't want to deal with individuals whose intention is to win at all points, or be declared "right" for the sake of being right. This makes the relationship confrontational rather than collaborative. The discussion becomes an argument, and the atmosphere turns tense. If you want to enhance your chances of winning someone over, be willing to consider ---and even agree upon ---reasonable requests. You may even volunteer to take losses in areas you can afford to give up, as long as you don't lose sight of the main goal.

A person who is willing to "give in" from time to time comes across as sensible and realistic. Moreover, concessions communicate a sincere desire to do what is best for another person. At the very least, it can promote a culture of "quid pro quo"; I will give you something, if you give me something in return.

The trick lies in choosing what you will concede. Understandably, you don't want to "give up" and concede the very thing you are selling. Keep sight of the main goal and judge what you can sacrifice based on this main goal. If you can create a win-win compromise between what you want and what the other person likes, better.

Consider this example:

How can you convince your boss to allow you to take freelance work outside your company --- something that you initially agreed not to do?

What if your boss tells you that you signed a contract that you will work exclusively for them, and that you taking freelance work outside the company will just result in a conflict of interest?

If you start opposing what your boss just said ---- for example you argue that they have never given you a single raise since you started five years ago and the economy has since changed ----- chances are, you'd just make your boss upset and defensive, decreasing your chances of influencing him or her.

However, if you concede that you did sign a contract (which you did!), and that yes, you can see how such a move can create a conflict of interest, then you can "mellow" your boss down.

This doesn't mean you've given up, however. You can follow your concession by presenting an alternative win-win proposal. How about a change in contract that states that you can't take freelance work from the company's main competitors, and that you're obliged to refer to the company any deal worth $5000 and above? The arrangement can give you the extra income you want, without the conflict of interest.

Bringing People to Your Side

In the previous module, we discussed the different ways you can increase your influence over other people, and set the stage for persuasion. We will continue on that thread in this module, and discuss the ways you can bring people to your side. Particularly, we will discuss the persuasive techniques of appealing to a person's emotions and reason.

A Dash of Emotion

Emotions have always been a driving force for people's behavior. Advertisers appeal to emotions all the time; they tell you that so-and-so beauty product can make you feel confident around the opposite sex, while so-and-so theme park can make you forget all your worries. There are those who begin a relationship based solely on how the other person made them feel. More so, advocacies, political campaigns, and even wars are waged, based on a collective sense of anger, contempt, or injustice.

Thus, you can never underestimate emotions as a way of influencing and persuading other people.

Why are emotions powerful? For one, emotions heavily influence a person's sense of comfort and general state of well-being. Positive emotions make us feel good, while negative emotions drive us to do something to make us feel good. But more so, emotions connect all of us to the "human" side of ourselves --- almost all emotions are universal and can cross race, religion, age, and social status.

How can you add a "dash of emotion" to your communication?

- Focus on positive emotions as benefits. If you want to bring a person to your side, tell them how good the proposal will make them feel. For example: if you want to convince your spouse to take you on that dream vacation, describe how relaxing a day you'll have. If he can picture it in his mind, then you've succeeded.

- Focus on a negative emotion, and then add a call to action. Negative emotions are powerful in influencing behavior because they bring about a sense of dissonance in a person. All people want to feel good, which is why anger, sadness, shock, or indignation doesn't sit well with most. An example of using a negative emotion to bring people to your side is describing the horror of an accident in order to convince people to wear their seat belts.

- Show that it's personal. Instead of focusing on the other person's emotions, you can focus on communicating your own. An effective way to persuade others is to show that your conviction is borne of a personal experience, and that you are emotionally attached to an idea. For example, showing your excitement verbally and non-verbally while explaining an ideal can show that you really believe in what you are pitching.

To be able to communicate emotion in your communication, you must use one of the influencing skills discussed earlier: seeing the other side. If you know how the other person looks at the situation, you will know what emotions will appeal to them.

Emotions can be communicated through body language (e.g. raising a fist to show that you are angry), variations in voice pitch, intonation and emphasis, directly saying what you feel or what you want the other person to feel, and painting a picture of situations where an emotional response is expected.

And don't forget: to use emotions effectively, use the appropriate amount. Less can be more, so don't overdo it!

Plenty of Facts

While emotions are a powerful influence to people's behavior, we all know that people are not just a bundle of emotions. Some situations require an appeal to the mind instead of the heart. An effective communication must make sense. More so, it must have basis in facts.

Facts create persuasive arguments because there is no way to dispute facts. If something is true, real, or verified by research, it has to be accepted. More so, presenting facts in communication show the extent that you have studied a subject, which in turn shows that you are serious in what you are saying.

There are two skills that can help in the use of facts during communication.

- The first skill is the ability to separate fact from opinion. Facts are objective data, and can be verified by credible procedures such as empirical research or expert opinion. It is considered true on the basis of actual evidence. An opinion, however, is a subjective statement that may be based on personal interpretation.

- The second skill is the ability to create logical arguments from facts. Facts can't be disputed, but you also have to use them properly in order to give them impact. Arguments from facts have to follow the rules of deductive or inductive reasoning. For example, from the research finding that watching TV increases attention deficiency among toddlers, "we should reduce TV time for toddlers" is a more valid conclusion than "attention deficiency doesn't exist in adults."

The following is an example of a communication that uses facts *"I believe I deserve this promotion because I was able to increase the department's productivity by 12% since I held office last year."*

Bringing It All Together

For best results, use both emotion and facts to influence people. After all, people use both their heart and mind in their daily lives, and addressing both is a more holistic approach to take.

The key is in being consistent, so that there isn't a dissonance between the emotional and the rational side of your communication. Done correctly, appeals to emotion can balance the coldness of reason, and facts can temper strong emotions.

Here is an example of a communication that has emotions and facts together:

"You should get that wedding dress! It makes you look like a princess --- think of how well it will flow when you walk down the aisle, the lights behind you. Plus, it's on sale --- 30% off. It fits your budget perfectly, leaving you with some extra cash to spend on accessories."

Chapter 5 – Sharing Your Opinion

In any social situation, you are expected to contribute. Sharing opinions is a way to present your personality to the world, and a way to create the image that you want to project. It is also an invitation for the other person to share their opinion, setting the stage for an engaging discussion or debate. In this module, we will discuss the skills you can use in sharing your opinion. Particularly, we will discuss how to use I-messages, disagree constructively, and build consensus.

Using I-Messages

An I-message is a message that is focused on the speaker. When you use I-messages, you take responsibility for your own feelings instead of accusing the other person of making you feel a certain way. The opposite of an I-message is a You-message.

An I-message is composed of the following:

A description of the problem or issue.

Describe the person's behavior you are reacting to in an objective, non-blameful, and non-judgmental manner.

"When ... "

Describe the concrete or tangible effects of that behavior.

"The effects are ... "

A suggestion for alternative behavior.

"I'd prefer ... "

Here is an example of an I-message:

"When I have to wait outside the office an extra hour because you didn't inform me that you'd be late (problem/issue), I become agitated (effect). I prefer for you to send me a message if you will not be able to make it (alternative behavior)."

The most important feature of I-messages is that they are neutral. There is no effort to threaten, argue, or blame in these statements.

You avoid making the other person defensive, as the essence of an I-message is "I have a problem" instead of "You have a problem". The speaker simply makes statements and takes full responsibility for his/her feelings.

Disagreeing Constructively

There is nothing wrong with disagreement. No two people are completely similar therefore it's inevitable that they would disagree on at least one issue. There's also nothing wrong in having a position and defending it.

To make the most of a disagreement, you have to keep it constructive. The following are some of the elements of a constructive disagreement:

- **Solution-focus.** The disagreement aims to find a workable compromise at the end of the discussion.

- **Mutual Respect.** Even if the two parties do not agree with one another, courtesy is always a priority.

- **Win-Win Solution.** Constructive disagreement is not geared towards getting the "one-up" on the other person. The premium is always on finding a solution that has benefits for both parties.

- **Reasonable Concessions.** More often than not, a win-win solution means you won't get your way completely. Some degree of sacrifice is necessary to meet the other person halfway. In constructive disagreement, parties are open to making reasonable concessions for the negotiation to move forward.

- **Learning-Focused.** Parties in constructive disagreement see conflicts as opportunities to get feedback on how well a system works, so that necessary changes can be made. They also see it as a challenge to be flexible and creative in coming up with solutions for everyone's gain.

Building Consensus

Consensus means unanimous agreement on an area of contention. Arriving at a consensus is the ideal resolution of bargaining. If both parties can find a solution that is agreeable to both of them, then anger can be prevented or reduced.

The following are some tips on how to arrive at a consensus:

- **Focus on interests rather than positions.** Surface the underlying value that makes people take the position they do. For example, the interest behind a request for a salary increase may be financial security. If you can communicate to the other party that you acknowledge this need, and will only offer a position that takes financial security into consideration, then a consensus is more likely to happen.

- **Explore options together.** Consensus is more likely if both parties are actively involved in the solution-making process. This ensures that there is increased communication about each party's positions. It also ensures that resistances are addressed.

- **Increase sameness and reduce differentiation.** A consensus is more likely if you can emphasize all the things that you and the other party have in common, and minimize all the things that make you different. An increased empathy can make finding common interests easier. It may also reduce psychological barriers to compromising. An example of increasing sameness and reducing differences is an employer and employee temporarily setting aside their position disparity and looking at the problem as two stakeholders in the same organization.

Chapter 6 – Negotiation Basics

We can do our best to persuade others to our side --- but what if the other party is as assertive? Then it's time for some bargaining! In this module we will discuss some basic negotiating skills that can help you in both getting the best deal for yourself, and engaging the other person into an amicable discussion. We will discuss negotiation in its four stages: preparation, opening, bargaining, and closing.

Preparation

Half the battle of negotiations is won during the preparation stage. Think of it as similar to strategizing before a war. You have to know ahead of time what the other side's strengths and weaknesses are, as well as your own. This will provide you with the knowledge on which approach to use.

The following are some tips in preparing for a negotiation:

Research what is standard for the area. To make sure that you don't get shortchanged, know the going rate for what you are offering or buying. For example, know what the standard salary is for a person with your background in a particular industry before going to a salary negotiation.

This advice may seem basic, but you'd be surprised at how many people actually forget to look in their backyards before a negotiation. Look for the strengths of your position and capitalize on them. Similarly, identify your weaknesses so that you can anticipate possible attacks.

Know your boundaries. This advice is related to the first one. As you study your interests and position, it is important to reflect ahead of time how much you are willing to concede, and what's non-negotiable for you. Having your boundaries clear in your mind will prevent you from making agreements that you'd regret later. It will also help you make the right amount of allowances for bargaining. Note though: don't dismiss the possibility that you might change your boundaries in the middle of the negotiation proper.

Step into their shoes. You know what's the best way to prepare a bargaining stance? Pretend to be the other party. Ask yourself: if you were the other side, what do you want to see or hear in order to give in?

If you can do extensive research about the players of the other party, as well as their position, better. Are you going to be dealing with people who are known to be difficult? Well, what makes them difficult? Do they have strong feelings about you? You can use information like these to help you plan your strategy.

Identify areas of bargaining. Now that you have studied your position, as well as the other side's position, it's now time to identify the common ground you can work on. A way to do this is to look for mutual interests. If you can emphasize that a move stands to benefit both parties in a satisfactory way, then you are more likely to get an agreement.

Prepare yourself mentally, emotionally and physically.
Negotiations can be a taxing endeavor. You need to be alert; in control and unemotional (but not emotionless) while you negotiate, so make sure you're in the right condition. In some cases, a lot of games and posturing will take place. So before going to the bargaining table, meditate, aim for a clear head, and get a good night's sleep.

Set up the time and venue for the negotiations. A significant element of negotiations is context. You have to make sure that the negotiation will be at a place and time when all parties feel at ease, as uncomfortable people are less likely to make concessions. This means you have to check even the tiny details of room temperature and space before you start a negotiation.

Moreover, you have to ensure that the seating arrangement is conducive to a friendly discussion. Two parties seating themselves from across each other may seem confrontational. Sitting too far away each other can send the message that you're not interested in finding common ground. Using dissimilar chairs can communicate a power play.

Opening

The way that you open a negotiation can set the tone for the whole bargaining session. It is important then that you pay attention to how you or the other party opens the negotiation.

The following are tips and techniques on opening a negotiation:

Express respect for the other party, and openness to the negotiation process. Negotiations have traditionally been perceived as a combative endeavor, but this need not be the case. In fact, simple courtesy can break the ice between two negotiating parties, and promote a reasonable discussion. So invest in pleasantries and small talk. Smile. At the end of the day, you are both just people with interests to pursue, and you can accomplish this without having to put anyone down.

Ask for more or higher than what you really want. Always assume that the other party will want to haggle with you, so ask for something greater than what you would be willing to accept. The excess is your bargaining allowance. Remember too, that the other party might just be willing to give you more than what you think you deserve, so there's nothing wrong with starting immodestly.

Don't accept the first offer. Keep in mind: the other party would expect you to haggle too! Chances are, you'd receive an initial offer lower than what a person or company is willing to give --- so invest in time convincing them you're worthy of more.

Put your strengths on the table. Here's a cardinal rule in negotiation: always negotiate from a position of strength. Don't beg or defend your weak points. Instead, illustrate from the onset the best about what you have to offer, and send the message that you're worth your asking

Bargaining

The heart of a negotiation process is the actual bargaining. There are times when bargaining is easy, especially if the meeting point of two positions does not require much sacrifice from either party. But there are also occasions when bargaining can be quite tedious. Negotiators can hold on to their stances stubbornly, either because they really don't think they can afford a concession, or they want you to be the one to yield.

The following are some tips to bargain more effectively:

Listen. Beginner negotiators are often more focused on what they want to say that they forget an important element of the process: listening. Take time to carefully listen to what the other party is saying to you; they can give you clues as to what is of value to them, and what counter-offer can make them give in. Similarly, note their non-verbal behavior to get clues regarding your pacing and demeanor.

Concede to get concessions. In the previous section, we discussed about the skill of "giving in without giving up." You can use this skill too during negotiations. Your concessions can be a way to sweeten the pot, or communicate to the other party that you also have their best interests at heart. For example: you can concede to lower the price of the goods you're selling, if they agree to buy a higher volume.

Anchor your position on objective data. This tip is related to the skill of using facts to bring people to your side. If you want to strengthen your bargaining position, make references to objective standards. For example, stating that you are offering a lower amount than the standard retail price of a good or service can strengthen your bargaining position.

Present options. Everyone likes to have a choice; it's empowering and keeps a person from feeling trapped. If you can afford it, create packages that the other party can choose from. You can win more if you have a "there's something for everyone approach."

Mind your phrasing. If you want something, make sure that it's phrased in such a way that is positive, and a benefit to the other party. For example, don't say that you want a higher salary because you have a graduate degree. Instead, say that your graduate degree can contribute positively to their bottom line. If you can show how your position furthers the other party's interest, then negotiations can proceed much more smoothly.

Closing

How you close a negotiation is as important as how you open one. You want to make sure that you leave the bargaining table with a satisfactory agreement for both sides. You also want to ensure that you end positively. After all, a settled deal means the possible start of a new relationship.

The following are some tips in closing the deal:

Be sensitive to signals that it's time to close. Always be sensitive to changes in the dynamics of the discussion, so that you will have fair warning that it's time to close. For example, the lessening of objections and counter arguments from the other party can be a sign that they have all the information that they need to make a decision. Similarly, requesting for a contract is an often signal that a decision has been made; all that's needed is to formalize it.

Here is some advice to consider before making a final offer. Haggling back and forth can take a while, but if you took the advice on setting boundaries before a negotiation, you'd know when you've reached your boundaries. If you sense that you are at that point of giving your final offer, and the other party seems to be as well, then issue a gentle but firm warning. For example, you can directly say "this is my final offer" or "I think I've reached a decision." The advice is a signal to the other party to give their final offer as well.

Increase the pressure. If the other party still seems hesitant, and you are ready to close the deal, then perhaps it's time to put pressure on them. Common ways to do this is to give a deadline to the offer ("This offer will expire by 2PM."), or showing that you have other options to consider ("I also have a proposal from XYZ company.")

Summarize. Another way to close a negotiation is to present a summary of what has been achieved so far, highlighting both the issues that have been resolved as well as what actions are expected of the participants so far. For instance you can say "we seem to agree on so-and-so details of the deal; we look forward to signing the contract tomorrow."

A summary is a positive way of ending a negotiation because it makes everyone feel that the time was well-spent. This is true even if the negotiation did not result in a mutually-agreed upon resolution. By emphasizing the idea that you moved forward despite lingering issues, you set the stage for further discussions.

Seal the commitment. Follow the ceremony that indicates a deal is formalized. Often this means signing the contract. In more informal settings, this can be a handshake. While they may seem like meaningless rituals, they are a sign of commitment to what has been agreed upon, and must be embraced warmly.

Thank. Lastly, end your negotiation with gratitude. Aside from observing the ethics of relationships, it shows your appreciation for the other party's time and consideration.

Chapter 7 – Making an Impact

Some people stand out, while others fade into the background. But if you want to make the most of interpersonal relationships, you have to be able to leave a lingering positive impression on the people that you meet. People's first impressions of you are what dictate if they want to get to know you any further. You want to make sure, then, that you create an impact on people.

Creating a Powerful First Impression

You've probably heard this saying before: *you don't get a second chance to make a first impression.*

In today's fast-paced world, you have to maximize the time and opportunities you get with the people that you meet. If you managed to secure a conference with a client or potential partner, for example, make sure that you don't leave anything to chance for that meeting. And that goes with the impression that you want to leave behind.

The following are some tips in creating a powerful first impression:

Dress to impress. Beauty is within, but this doesn't mean that people don't make conclusions about you based on your appearance. If you want to create a great first impression make sure that you look your best. Whenever you're presenting yourself to other people, be clean, well-groomed and dressed in clothes that fit and within the prescribed dress code

Be positive. Nobody likes to talk to cranky, irritable, and pessimistic people! Instead, people are drawn to those who smile a lot and radiate a pleasant disposition. If you want to be remembered, make them feel welcomed and appreciated. A positive experience is as easy to remember as a negative one!

Communicate your confidence. Powerful first impressions are those that show you are self-assured, competent, and purposive. Always establish eye contact with the people you are talking to. Shake hands firmly. Speak in a deliberate and purposive way.

Be yourself! Meeting people for the first time can be extremely anxiety-provoking, but do your best to act naturally. People are more responsive to those who don't come across as if they're putting on a front or are very controlled. Let your personality engage the other person.

Go for the extra mile. Do more than the usual that can make you stand out from the rest. For example, if you're going for a job interview, show that you studied the company very well and know their mission and vision. If others can see that you appreciation a social situation, they are more likely to remember you positively.

Assessing a Situation

All interpersonal skills involve sensitivity to what is going on around, especially what is happening with the people you are interacting with. After all, context variables, such as timing and location, can change the meaning of a communication. You want to make sure that you are not just saying the right thing, but you are saying the right thing at the right moment.

If you want to make an impact, you have to factor in the situation.

The following are some tips in assessing the situation:

Listen, not just to what is being said, but also to what is NOT being said. An excellent interpersonal skill to master is a keen observing eye. You have to be able to note the body language of the people around you in order for you to be able to respond appropriately. For example, there is body language that says *"go on, we like what you're saying."* There is also body language that says *"I don't want to hear that right now."*

Identify needs. A second way to assess the situation is to ask yourself: what does this social occasion need right now? A newly formed group, for example, likely has members who still don't know one another. The need then is for someone to help break the ice. A group that is tired from a long working day probably needs an opportunity to relax and unwind. Knowing these needs can help you respond to them more appropriately.

Practice etiquette. Etiquette may seem like a useless bunch of rules to some people but they serve a purpose: they tell you what are generally considered as acceptable and unacceptable for certain situations. It helps then that you know basic etiquette rules so that you don't make a faux pas that can ruin the great first impression that you made.

Being Zealous without Being Offensive

Enthusiasm, diligence, and persistence are all great virtues to have, especially if you're in the business of creating social networks. However, you have to be careful that your persevering doesn't cross the line to pestering --- or worse harassing the person.

The following are some tips in being zealous without being offensive:

Focus on what is important to the other person. Being "other-centered" is the best way to monitor your own eagerness to make contact with other people. Before you do something, make that habit of asking yourself: does this action address the need of the other person, or is it merely addressing my need?

Respect boundaries. Everyone has personal boundaries, and it would do us well to respect them. Not seeing clients without an appointment is an example of a boundary. The same goes for not accepting calls during the weekend or past regular office hours. Work within these boundaries, and you'll be able to communicate your courtesy. And if you don't know what a person's boundaries are, you have nothing to lose in asking!

Make requests, not demands. As mentioned previously, we can always do our best to persuade and influence other people, but we can't force them to do what they don't want to do. So always courteously ask for permission, and verify agreement. And if they say no ---- then accept the no as an answer, unless you have something new to offer.

Note non-verbal behavior. Similar to the tip in the previous section, always be guided by the other person's non-verbal response to you. If you find that they are already showing irritation --- example they speak in a gruff, annoyed tone when talking to you ---- then perhaps it's time to back off. But if they appear open to you --- they look at you with interest while you speak --- then it's advisable to go on.

Additional Titles

The 90 Minute Guide series of books covers a variety of general business skills and are intended to be completed in 90 minutes or less. It is an effective way for building your skill set and can be used to acquire professional development units needed by project managers and other industries to maintain their certification. For the availability of titles please see

https://www.silvercitypublications.com/shop/.

No. 1 - Appreciative Inquiry

No. 2 - Assertiveness and Self Control

No. 3 - Attention Management

No. 4 - Body Language Basics

No. 5 - Business Acumen

No. 6 - Business and Etiquette

No. 7 - Change Management

No. 8 - Coaching and Mentoring

No. 9 - Communications Strategies

No. 10 - Conflict Resolution

No. 11 - Creative Problem Solving

No. 12 - Delivering Constructive Criticism

No. 13 - Developing Creativity

No. 14 - Developing Emotional Intelligence

No. 15 - Developing Interpersonal Skills

No. 16 - Developing Social Intelligence

No. 17 - Employee Motivation

No. 18 - Facilitation Skills

No. 19 - Goal Setting and Getting Things Done

No. 20 - Knowledge Management Fundamentals

No. 21 - Leadership and Influence

No. 22 - Lean Process and Six Sigma Basics

No. 23 - Managing Anger

No. 24 - Meeting Management

No. 25 - Negotiation Skills

No. 26 - Networking Inside a Company

No. 27 - Networking Outside a Company

No. 28 - Office Politics for Managers

No. 29 - Organizational Skills

No. 30 - Performance Management

No. 31 - Presentation Skills

No. 32 - Public Speaking

No. 33 - Servant Leadership

No. 34 - Team Building for Management

No. 35 - Team Work and Team Building

No. 36 - Time Management

No. 37 - Top 10 Soft Skills You Need

No. 38 - Virtual Team Building and Management

www.ingramcontent.com/pod-product-compliance
Lightning Source LLC
Chambersburg PA
CBHW060647280326
41933CB00012B/2181